CONT

I I
PSALMS OF SORROW TO GOD

PART TWO: PSALMS OF PRAISE
III
PSALMS OF PRAISE TO HUMANKIND

FOREWORD

The words of the psalms are like breath, like yeast that gets kneaded into the dough of consciousness. Taped to my exercise machine is a snippet from Psalm 36. I memorize the words as I move my arms and legs. I work them into my muscles and sinews.

Your love, God, reaches to heaven;
your truth to the skies.
Your justice is like God's mountain,
your judgments like the deep.
(Ps. 36)

I savor the words. I sip them like fine liqueur.

I've been learning the psalms since I was a child. Once they're inside you, and you know them by heart, they well up when you need them, or you can draw them up at will from the deep well of your soul. When I was in the death house with Robert Lee Willie, who was facing execution in Louisiana's electric chair, it was Psalm 51 that welled up:

A clean heart create in me, O God,
and a steadfast spirit renew within me . . .
for you are not pleased with sacrifices . . .
a heart contrite and humbled you will
not spurn. . . .

During my novitiate days after our mid-day examination of conscience we prayed Psalm 51 as we walked to lunch. Then, there it was in the death house. Words for him. Words for me. Words that were like a rope I could grab and hold. Words that cleansed me and gave me courage.

This snippet from Psalm 36 is also in front of my eyes when I exercise:

*they drink from the stream of your
delight.*

Isn't praying this and similar psalms of praise like thrusting your face into a swift stream? Isn't it like taking pure sips of God's sustaining love? I drink from these streams again and again. I drink from the stream of friendship and I drink from the presence of the most poor, despised people on earth. I find a pure drink of Christ in the inner city and in prison cells and on death row. The stream is not always delight. But always, there is that mysterious joy that comes from being in the presence of God.

But there are times when the last thing we want to hear is about joy and delight and the comfort of God's presence. When we have been hurt or others we love have been hurt or when we've been terribly wronged or lied about or assaulted, we need the words to belt out our lament. We need to moan unrestrained, to complain without censure. We need to put the dregs of bitterness and hatred out there in front of God.

I'm glad that this little book of selected psalms is being published. It's small enough to tuck into our suitcases or keep by our bedside or in our cars. Waiting in a parking lot or even at a stoplight, we can sip from this abundant stream. And if we learn these soul-cries by heart, we can drink from them any time we want.

Sister Helen Prejean, csj,
Author of Dead Man Walking

PREFACE

*T*he impetus for this book grew out of my love of reading the Psalms aloud. It represents my effort to select, arrange, and edit various poetical texts of the Bible into unified psalms for oral reading. Although most of these psalms are new in the sense that they are composites of various texts, they are totally Biblical in imagery and sentiment. (See "Reading the Psalms" on page 83.) They also preserve the basic literary device used by Biblical poets, which is the couplet.

The couplet in Biblical poetry consists of two unrhymed but complementary lines or expressions—a technique usually referred to by scholars as parallelism. Often the two lines of a couplet say the same thing but in different words, as the following example demonstrates:

> *Why are you cast down, O my soul,*
> *and why are you disquieted within me?*
> *(Ps 42:5)*

Biblical poetry does occasionally diverge from the traditional use of the couplet. One variant consists of verses containing units of three lines each. Psalm 100 consistently follows this pattern. There are also poetical passages that simply don't use parallelism as a device (Ps 90:1-2, for example).

For the most part, I composed the new psalms of this book by re-arranging couplets or clusters of couplets as they occur in the Biblical text. Occasionally, I have reversed the order of the lines of a couplet. And I have also created new couplets by joining single lines from two different texts to form a new verse. I used the New Revised Standard Version as the source of these psalms.

There is nothing final or definitive about the psalms I have selected, arranged, and edited in this collection. For me, they are an additional way to appreciate the spiritual poetry of the Bible. They nourish my own aesthetic and spiritual sensibilities, and I trust that others will find sustenance in them.

Frederick W. Bassett

ACKNOWLEDGMENTS

With grateful appreciation, I acknowledge my indebtedness to a host of individuals who have enriched my life with love, friendship, wisdom, knowledge, wit, narration, and trust. I give special thanks to my sons, Jonathan and Michael; my parents, Mary Barsh Bassett and the late Leon Frederick Bassett; my other parents, John Wallace Roberts and the late Vennie Lee Roberts; my sisters and brothers, Sara, George, Martha, Paul, Lynda, Diane, Kathy, John, and Joan; my all-but siblings, Myra, Betty, Travis, and Donald; my dear friends, Faye and Preston Edwards, Jo Faddis, June Foster, Peg Hamilton, Catherine and David Hawkins, Scott Houston, Eleanor and Guy Meredith, Gail and Jimmy Moss, and Brewster Robertson; and two notable mentors, Martin Buss and J. J. Owens.

PART ONE

Psalms of Sorrow

When I lie down I say,
"When shall I rise?"

—Job 7:4

I

PSALMS OF SORROW TO HUMANKIND

Is It Nothing to You, All You Who Pass By?

1 Is it nothing to you,
   all you who pass by?
   Look at me and be appalled.
2 I am shaken off like a locust;
   I am gone like a shadow at evening.

3 There is no soundness in my flesh;
   there is no health in my bones.
4 I am utterly bowed down
   and prostrate;
   all day long I go around mourning.

5 I have sewed sackcloth upon my skin,
   and have laid my strength in the dust.
6 Is it nothing to you,
   all you who pass by?
   Look at me and be appalled.

My Heart Is Like Wine That Has No Vent

1 My heart is like wine
   that has no vent;
   like new wineskins,
   it is ready to burst.
2 I must speak,
   so that I may find relief;
   for I have passed out of mind
   like one who is dead.

3 I live as an alien in the land;
   no one cares for me.
4 I am loathsome to my own family;
   my relatives have failed me.

5 All my intimate friends abhor me,
   and those whom I love
   have turned against me.
6 My acquaintances
   are estranged from me;
   the guests in my house
   have forgotten me.

7 My companions are treacherous
   like a torrent-bed,
   like freshets that pass away.
8 In time of heat they disappear;
   when it is hot,
   they vanish from their place.

⁹ I looked for pity,
  but there was none;
  for comforters, but I found none.
¹⁰ My lyre is turned to mourning,
  and my pipe to the voice
  of those who weep.

When I Waited for Light, Darkness Came

¹ Oh, that I were
   as in the months of old,
   as in the days
   when God watched over me,
² when his lamp shone over my head,
   and by his light
   I walked through darkness.

³ I delivered the poor who cried,
   and the orphan who had no helper.
⁴ The blessing of the wretched
   came upon me,
   and I caused the widow's heart
   to sing for joy.

⁵ I was eyes to the blind,
   and feet to the lame.
⁶ I was a father to the needy,
   and I championed
   the cause of the stranger.

⁷ My roots spread out to the waters,
   with the dew all night
   on my branches;
⁸ my glory was fresh with me,
   and my bow ever new in my hand.

9 Now my soul
   is poured out within me;
   days of affliction
   have taken hold of me.
10 My inward parts are never still,
   and I go about in sunless gloom.

11 Did I not weep
   for those whose day was hard?
   Was not my soul
   grieved for the poor?
12 But when I looked for good,
   evil came;
   when I waited for light,
   darkness came.

Truly the Thing I Fear Comes upon Me

1 Truly the thing I fear comes upon me,
   and what I dread befalls me.
2 For I know that God
   will bring me to death,
   to the house appointed for all living.
3 My days are swifter
   than a weaver's shuttle
   and come to their end without hope.

4 There is hope for a tree,
   if it is cut down,
   that it will sprout again.
5 Though its root grows old in the earth,
   and its stump dies in the ground,
6 yet at the scent of water it will bud
   and put forth branches
   like a young plant.

7 But mortals die, and are laid low;
   humans expire, and where are they?
8 As waters fail from a lake,
   and a river wastes away and dries up,
9 so mortals lie down
   and do not rise again;
   until the heavens are no more,
   they will not awake.

10 As the cloud fades and vanishes,
   so those who go down to Sheol
   do not come up.
11 They return no more to their houses,
   nor do their places
   know them any more.
12 Their children come to honor,
   and they do not know it;
   they are brought low,
   and it goes unnoticed.

13 So I am consigned
   to the gates of Sheol;
   I shall look upon mortals no more.
14 Though my flesh and my heart fail,
   God is my portion forever.
15 In the Lord I take refuge;
   into his hand I commend my spirit.

O That My Vexation Were Weighed

1 O that my vexation were weighed,
   and all my calamity
   laid in the balance.
2 It would be heavier
   than the sand of the sea;
   therefore, I will not restrain my mouth.
   I will speak in the anguish of my spirit;
   I will complain
   in the bitterness of my soul.

3 Wretched and close to death
   from my youth up,
   I suffer God's terrors;
   I am desperate.
4 Day and night his hand
   is heavy upon me;
   my strength is dried up
   by the heat of summer.
5 Evils have encompassed me
   without number;
   they are more
   than the hairs of my head.

6 If I speak, my pain is not assuaged;
   if I forbear, how much of it leaves me?
7 My groanings
   are poured out like water;
   my eye has grown dim from grief.
8 O that I might see some good,
   that I might smile before I depart.

My Days Are Past,
My Plans Are Broken Off

¹ Have pity on me,
  O you my friends,
  for the hand of God has touched me!
² The arrows of the almighty are in me;
  my spirit drinks their poison.
³ I am shut in so that I cannot escape;
  my eye will never again see good.

⁴ Have pity on me,
  O you my friends,
  for the hand of God has touched me!
⁵ He has walled up my way
  so that I cannot pass,
  and he has set darkness
  upon my paths.
⁶ My days are swifter than a runner;
  they flee away, they see no good.

⁷ Have pity on me,
  O you my friends,
  for the hand of God has touched me!
⁸ He has stripped my glory from me,
  and taken the crown from my head.
⁹ My honor is pursued as by the wind,
  and my prosperity
  has passed away like a cloud.

10 Have pity on me,
    O you my friends,
    for the hand of God has touched me!
11 He has broken me down
    on every side;
    he has uprooted my hope like a tree.
12 My joy is gone,
    my heart is sick;
    my days are past,
    my plans are broken off.

My Eyes Are Weary from Looking Up

1 Hear my words, you wise men;
   and give ear to me,
   you who know.
2 Why does the way of the guilty prosper?
   Why do all who are treacherous thrive?

3 Those greedy for gain curse the Lord;
   with their mouths
   they speak arrogantly.
4 They make their tongue sharp as a snake's;
   under their lips is the venom of vipers.

5 Evil is in their homes
   and in their hearts;
   they flatter themselves in their own eyes.
6 They do not speak peace,
   but they conceive deceitful words.

7 Their hearts are fat and gross;
   they hold fast to their evil purpose.
8 Each evening they come back,
   howling like dogs
   and prowling about.

9 They sit in ambush in the villages;
   they seize the poor
   and drag them off.
10 They kill the widow and the stranger;
   they murder the orphan.

11 The tents of robbers are at peace,
   and those who provoke God are secure.
12 When I cry, "Violence!"
   I am not answered;
   I call aloud, but there is no justice.

13 Hear my words, you wise men;
   give ear to me,
   all you who know.
14 How long will the land mourn?
   My eyes are weary from looking upward.

How Lonely Sits the City

1 How lonely sits the city
   that once was full of people!
   How like a widow she has become,
   she that was great among the nations!

2 All her people groan
   as they search for bread;
   they trade their treasures for food
   to revive their strength.

3 Those who feasted on delicacies
   perish in the streets;
   those who were brought up in purple
   cling to ash heaps.

4 The tongue of the infant sticks
   to the roof of its mouth for thirst;
   the children beg for food,
   but no one gives them anything.

5 In the street the sword bereaves;
   in the house it is like death.
6 How the gold has grown dim!
   How the pure gold is changed!

In the Noontide of My Days I Must Depart

1 O my heart is in anguish,
   for the terrors of death
   have fallen upon me.
2 Fear and trembling come upon me;
   and horror overwhelms me.

3 I am counted among those
   who go down to the Pit;
   I am like those who have no help,
4 like those forsaken among the dead,
   like the slain that lie in the grave.

5 I waited for light,
   and lo! there is darkness;
   searched for brightness,
   but I walk in gloom.
6 I stumble at noon as in the twilight,
   among the vigorous
   as though I were dead.

7 In the noontide of my days
   I must depart;
   like a weaver I have rolled up my life.
8 Now I shall lie in the earth;
   you shall seek me,
   but I shall not be here.

The Grave Is Ready for Me

1 Why is light given to one in misery,
and life to the bitter in soul,
2 who long for death,
but it does not come,
and dig for it more than
for hidden treasures;
3 who rejoice exceedingly,
and are glad when they find the grave?

4 There the wicked cease from troubling,
and there the weary are at rest.
5 There the prisoners are at ease together;
they do not hear
the voice of the taskmaster.
6 The small and the great are there,
and the slaves are free
from their masters.

7 O that I might have my request,
and that God would grant my desire;
8 that it would please God to crush me,
that he would let loose his hand
and cut me off!
9 I would even exult in unrelenting pain;
for I have not denied
the words of the Holy One.

10 What is my strength,
 that I should wait?
 And what is my end,
 that I should be patient?
11 In truth I have no help in me,
 and any resource is driven from me.
12 My spirit is broken,
 my days are extinct,
 the grave is ready for me.

II
PSALMS OF SORROW TO GOD

How Long, O Lord? How Long?

1 How long, O Lord? How long?
    How long must I bear pain in my soul?
2 Every day I call on you, O Lord;
    I spread out my hands to you.

3 For I am severely afflicted;
    I am utterly spent and crushed.
4 My days are like an evening shadow;
    I wither away like grass.

5 My bones burn like a furnace,
    and my eyes grow dim through sorrow.
6 The joy of my heart has ceased;
    I have forgotten what happiness is.

7 Do the beasts of burden bray
    over their grass,
    or the oxen low over their fodder?
8 Answer me, O Lord my God!
    or I will sleep the sleep of death.

9 Heal me, O Lord,
  and I shall be healed;
  save me, and I shall be saved.
10 You are the God of my salvation;
  for you I wait all day long.

Have Mercy upon Me, O God

1 Have mercy upon me, O God,
   according to your steadfast love;
   according to your abundant mercy,
   blot out my transgressions.

2 For I know my transgressions,
   and my sin is ever before me.
3 O God, my iniquities
   have gone over my head like a yoke;
   they weigh like a burden
   too heavy upon me.

4 All day long my disgrace
   is before me, O God,
   and shame has covered my face.
5 Dread has come upon me,
   and trembling,
   which makes all my bones shake.

6 O Lord, do not rebuke me
   in your anger,
   or discipline me in your wrath.
7 Do not cast me away
   from your presence,
   and do not take
   your holy spirit from me.

8 If I were to give a burnt offering,
  you would not be pleased.
9 But a broken and contrite heart
  you will not despise.

10 Wash me thoroughly
  from my iniquity,
  and cleanse me from my sin.
11 Purge me with hyssop,
  and I shall be clean;
  wash me, O God,
  and I shall be whiter than snow.

To You, O Lord, I Lift Up My Soul

1 To you, O Lord, I lift up my soul;
   O my God, in you I trust.
2 Out of the depths
   I cry to you, O my God;
   to you I lift up my eyes.

3 For I have come into deep waters,
   and the flood sweeps over me.
4 Trouble and anguish
   have come upon me, O Lord,
   and my soul melts away for sorrow.

5 Be not far from me, O Lord,
   for there is no one to help.
6 Stretch out your hand from on high
   and rescue me from mighty waters.

7 For you alone, O Lord,
   my soul waits in silence;
   you alone are my rock
   and my salvation.
8 My soul waits for you, O Lord,
   more than those
   who wait for the morning.

9 O Lord, lead me to the rock
  that is higher than I,
  for you are my refuge.
10 Let me abide in your tent forever;
  let me find refuge, O my God,
  under the shadow of your wings.

My God, My God,
Why Have You Forsaken Me?

1 My God, my God,
   why have you forsaken me?
   Why are you so far
   from helping me?
2 O my God, I cry by day,
   but you do not answer;
   and by night, but find no rest.
3 For the snares of death
   encompass me,
   and the pangs of Sheol
   lay hold on me.

4 I am poured out like water;
   all my bones are out of joint.
   My heart is like wax;
   it is melted within my breast.
5 My mouth is dried up
   like a broken jar,
   and my tongue sticks to my jaw.

6 I stretch out my hand for you;
   my soul thirsts for you
   like a parched land.
7 It was you, O God,
   who took me from the womb;
   you kept me safe
   on my mother's breast.

8 On you I was cast from my birth;
  since my mother bore me
  you have been my God.

9 Do not hide your face from me,
  and do not forsake me,
  O God of my salvation.
10 Let my prayer
  be counted as incense,
  the lifting up of my hands
  as a sacrifice.
11 O my God, do not be far away!
  O my help, come quickly to my aid!

Rise Up, O Lord

1 Rise up, O Lord!
   Do not let mortals prevail;
   incline your ear to me,
   hear my words.
2 Look, the wicked bend the bow;
   they have fitted
   their arrow to the string.

3 See how they conceive evil,
   and are pregnant with mischief.
4 On every side the wicked prowl,
   as vileness is exalted
   among humankind.

5 Their mouths are filled
   with cursing and deceit;
   under their tongues
   are mischief and iniquity.
6 All their thoughts are,
   "There is no God";
   they think in their hearts,
   "We shall not be moved."

7 In arrogance the wicked
   persecute the poor;
   their eyes watch for the helpless.
8 They lurk in secret
   like a lion in its covert;
   in hiding places
   they murder the innocent.

9 Why, O lord,
   do you stand far off?
   Why do you hide yourself
   in times of trouble?
10 O let the evil of the wicked
   come to an end;
   let the net that they hid
   ensnare them.

11 Rise up, O Lord,
   lift up your hand;
   break the arm of the evildoers.
12 Let them vanish
   like water that runs away;
   like grass let them
   be trodden down and wither.

My Spirit Fails

1 Give ear to my words, O Lord;
   give heed to my sighing.
2 Hear the voice of my supplication;
   turn to me, O lord, and save my life.

3 My bones burn with heat;
   my belly is in turmoil.
4 My soul is full of trouble,
   and my life draws near to Sheol.

5 When I think of it I am dismayed,
   and shuddering seizes my flesh.
6 My face is red with weeping,
   and deep darkness is on my eyelids.

7 Give ear to my words, O Lord,
   give heed to my sighing.
8 Answer me quickly, O Lord;
   my spirit fails.

In the Shadow of Your Wings

1 In you, O Lord, I seek refuge;
   O my God, do not be far from me.
2 Turn to me and be gracious to me,
   for I am lonely and afflicted.

3 My soul is cast down within me,
   and my heart is withered like grass.
4 My life is spent with sorrow,
   and my years with sighing.

5 Like a slave who longs for the shadows,
   like laborers who look for their wages,
6 so I am allotted months of emptiness,
   and nights of misery
   are appointed for me.

7 When I lie down I say,
   "When shall I rise?"
   For I am full of tossing until dawn.
8 I am weary with my moaning;
   my eyes waste away because of grief.

9 Be merciful to me, O God,
   be merciful to me,
   for in you my soul takes refuge;
   in the shadow of your wings
   I will take refuge,
   until the storms pass by.

O Lord, How Long Shall the Wicked

¹ O Lord, how long shall the wicked,
   how long shall the wicked exult?
² I am distraught
   by the noise of the enemy,
   because of the clamor of the wicked.

³ They scoff and speak with malice;
   they set their mouths against heaven.
⁴ Their hearts overflow with follies;
   violence covers them like a garment.

⁵ I see violence and strife in the city;
   iniquity and trouble are within it.
⁶ Ruin is in its midst;
   oppression and fraud do not depart.

⁷ Justice is turned back,
   and righteousness stands at a distance;
   truth stumbles in the public square,
   and uprightness cannot enter.

⁸ O that I had wings like a dove!
   I would fly away and be at rest.
⁹ Truly, I would flee far away;
   I would lodge in the wilderness.

10 O Lord, how long shall the wicked,
  how long shall the wicked exult?
11 I am distraught
  by the noise of the enemy,
  because of the clamor of the wicked.

I Would Not Live Forever

1 Surely now, O God,
  you have worn me out;
  you have made desolate
  all my company.

2 You lift me up on the wind
  and toss me about
  in the roar of the storm.

3 My eye has grown dim,
  and all my members
  are like a shadow.

4 The night racks my bones,
  and the pain that gnaws me
  takes no rest.

5 Is my strength
  the strength of stones,
  or is my flesh bronze?

6 My heart throbs,
  my strength fails me;
  my soul is forlorn.

7 I would choose death
  rather than this body;
  I loathe my life;
  I would not live forever.

Teach Us to Number Our Days

1 In all generations, O God,
   you have been our dwelling place.
2 Before the mountains
   were brought forth,
   or ever you had formed
   the earth and the world,
   from everlasting to everlasting
   you are God.
3 A thousand years in your sight
   are like yesterday when it is past,
   or like a watch in the night.

4 But the days of our life
   are seventy years,
   or perhaps eighty, if we are strong;
   even then their span
   is toil and trouble;
   they are soon gone, and we fly away.

5 We are like a dream
   or like grass in the morning.
6 In the morning it flourished;
   in the evening it fades and withers.
7 So our years come to an end,
   and you turn us back to dust.
   You say, "Turn back, you mortals,"
   and you sweep us away.

8 So teach us to number our days
   that we may gain a wise heart.

O Prosper the Work of My Hands

1 Turn, O Lord! How Long?
   Have compassion on your servant!
2 For I am consumed by your anger;
   by your wrath I am overwhelmed.

3 My strength fails
   and my bones waste away, O God;
   night and day, my tears
   have been my food.
4 All my days pass away
   under your wrath;
   my years come to an end like a sigh.

5 O my God, in you I take refuge;
   my times are in your hand.
6 Satisfy me in the morning
   with your steadfast love
   so that I may rejoice
   and be glad all my days.
7 O Lord my God, let your work
   be manifest to your servant;
   let your favor be upon me,
   and prosper the work of my hands—
   O prosper the work of my hands!

O Lord, All My Longing
Is Known to You

1 O Lord, all my longing
is known to you;
my sighing is not hidden from you.
2 Make me to know your ways,
for I have gone astray
like a lost sheep.

3 O Lord, restore to me
the joy of your salvation,
and sustain in me a willing spirit.
4 O send out your light and truth;
let them bring me to your holy hill.

5 Teach me wisdom, O God,
in my secret heart,
for you have no delight in sacrifice.
6 Create in me a clean heart
and put a right spirit within me.

7 Let the words of my mouth
and the meditations of my heart
be acceptable to you,
O Lord, my rock and my redeemer.
8 It is for you, O Lord, that I wait;
it is you, O Lord my God,
who will answer.
9 As a deer longs for flowing streams,
so my soul longs for you, O Lord.

O Lord, You Have Searched Me
and Know Me

1 O Lord, you have searched me
   and know me;
   you know when I sit down
   and when I rise up.
2 You discern my thoughts
   from far away,
   and are acquainted with all my ways.

3 If I have raised my hand
   against the orphan,
   or have caused the eye
   of the widow to fail,
4 be gracious to me, O Lord,
   and forgive all my sins.

5 If I have seen anyone perish
   for lack of clothing,
   or a poor person without covering,
6 be gracious to me, O Lord,
   and forgive all my sins.

7 If I have rejoiced at the ruin
   of those who hate me,
   or exulted when evil overtook them,
8 be gracious to me, O Lord,
   and forgive all my sins.

⁹ If I have walked with falsehood,
   or my foot has hurried to deceit,
¹⁰ be gracious to me, O Lord,
   and forgive all my sins.

¹¹ If my step has turned aside
   from the way,
   or my heart has followed
   after my eye,
¹² be gracious to me, O Lord,
   and forgive all my sins.

¹³ Answer me, O God of my right,
   hear my prayer,
¹⁴ and deliver me
   from all my transgressions,
   for my hope is in you.

PART TWO

Psalms of Praise

O come let us sing to the Lord; let us
make a joyful noise to the rock of our
salvation!

—Psalm 95:1

III
PSALMS OF PRAISE TO HUMANKIND

O Come, Let Us Sing to the Lord

1 O come, let us sing to the Lord;
   let us make a joyful noise
   to the rock of our salvation!
2 Let us come into his presence
   with thanksgiving;
   let us make a joyful noise to him
   with songs of praise!

3 For the Lord is faithful
   in all his words,
   and gracious in all his deeds.
4 He is near to all who call on him,
   to all who call on him in truth.

5 His steadfast love
   is as high as the heavens;
   his faithfulness extends to the clouds.
6 When deeds of iniquity overwhelm us,
   he forgives our transgressions.

7 O magnify the Lord with me,
   and let us exalt his name together.
8 Blessed be the Lord forever.
   Amen and Amen.

The Lord Is My Shepherd

1 The Lord is my shepherd;
 I shall not want.

2 He makes me lie
 down in green pastures;
 he leads me beside still waters.

3 He restores my soul;
 he leads me in paths of righteousness
 for his name's sake.

4 Even though I walk
 through the darkest valley,
 I will fear no evil;
 for he is with me;
 his rod and his staff—
 they comfort me.

5 He prepares a table before me
 in the presence of my enemies;
 he anoints my head with oil;
 my cup overflows.

6 Surely, goodness and mercy
 shall follow me
 all the days of my life,
 and I shall dwell
 in the house of the Lord
 my whole life long.

Make a Joyful Noise to the Lord

1 Make a joyful noise to the Lord;
   worship the Lord with gladness;
   come into his presence with singing.

2 Praise him with the lyre;
   make melody to him with the harp;
   play the strings, with loud shouts.

3 Know that the Lord is God;
   it is he that made us,
   and we are his people.

4 Yea the heavens are his;
   the earth also is his;
   the world and all that is in it.

5 Enter his gates with thanksgiving,
   and his courts with praise;
   give thanks to him, bless his name.

6 For the Lord is good;
   his steadfast love endures forever,
   his faithfulness to all generations.

O Seek the Lord and His Strength

1 O seek the Lord and his strength;
  seek his presence continually.
2 For all his precepts
  are trustworthy;
   they are established forever and ever.
3 The unfolding
  of his words give light;
   it imparts understanding to the simple.

4 Happy are those
  whose way is blameless,
  who walk in the law of the Lord,
5 who do not follow
  the advice of the wicked,
  or take the path that sinners tread.
6 Their delight is in the law of the Lord,
  and on his law
  they meditate day and night.

7 O seek the Lord and his strength;
  seek his presence continually.
8 For with the Lord
  there is steadfast love;
  with him is great power to redeem.
9 The Lord is gracious and merciful;
  his compassion
  is over all that he has made.

10 Happy are those
   who observe justice,
   who do righteousness at all times,
11 who make the Lord their trust,
   who do not go astray
   after false gods.
12 Their delight is in the law of the Lord,
   and on his law
   they meditate day and night.

The Lord Is My Chosen Portion

1 The Lord is my chosen portion;
    he is my strength and my might.
2 I will bless the Lord at all times;
    his praise shall be in my mouth.

3 Though the fig tree does not blossom
    and no fruit is on the vines,
    yet I will give thanks to the Lord,
    I will sing praises to him.

4 Though the produce of the olive fails
    and the fields yield no food,
    yet I will praise the name of God,
    I will magnify him with thanksgiving.

5 Though the flock is cut off from the fold
    and there is no herd in the stalls,
    yet I will rejoice in the Lord,
    I will exult in the God of my salvation.

Praise the Lord

1 Praise the Lord;
   Praise him for his mighty deeds!
2 Praise the Lord;
   Praise him according to his greatness!

3 Praise the Lord from the heavens;
   Praise him from the earth!
4 Praise the Lord in his sanctuary;
   Praise him in his mighty firmament!

5 Praise the Lord, all his angels;
   Praise him, all his host!
6 Praise the Lord, sun and moon;
   Praise him, all you shining stars!

7 Praise the Lord, all peoples;
   Praise him, men and women alike!
8 Praise the Lord, all peoples;
   Praise him, old and young together!

9 Praise the Lord with trumpet;
   Praise him with lute and harp!
10 Praise the Lord with tambourine;
   Praise him with strings and pipe!

¹¹ Praise the Lord;
   Praise him for his mighty deeds!
¹² Praise the Lord;
   Praise him according to his greatness!

God Is King of All the Earth

¹ Clap your hands, all you people;
  shout to God
  with loud songs of joy.
² For the Lord, the Most High,
  is awesome,
  a great king over all the earth.

³ In his hands
  are the depths of the earth;
  the heights of the mountains
  are his also.
⁴ He has fixed
  all the bounds of the earth;
  he made summer and winter.

⁵ His is the day,
  his also the night;
  he established the luminaries
  and the sun.
⁶ He crowns the year
  with his bounty;
  the pastures
  of the wilderness overflow.

7 The meadows
  clothe themselves with flocks;
  the valleys deck
  themselves with grain.
8 The hills gird themselves with joy;
  they shout and sing together.

9 Clap your hands, all you people;
  shout to God
  with loud songs of joy.
10 For God sits on his holy throne;
  God is king of all the earth.

This Is the Day the Lord Has Made

1 This is the day the Lord has made;
  let us rejoice and be glad in it.
2 Let those who fear the Lord say,
  "His steadfast love endures forever."

3 How precious is God's steadfast love!
  All people may take refuge
  in the shadow of his wings.
4 They feast on the abundance of his house,
  and he gives them drink
  from the river of his delights.

5 Happy are the people
  who know the festal shout,
  who walk in the light of his countenance;
6 they exult in his name all day long,
  and extol his righteousness.

7 He is the glory of their strength;
  by his favor their horn is exalted.
8 When deeds of iniquity
  overwhelm them,
  he forgives their transgressions.

9 Let the redeemed of the Lord say so,
  those he redeemed from trouble.
10 O give thanks to the Lord,
  for he is good;
  his steadfast love endures forever.

ಌ 53 ಜ

O Taste and See That the Lord Is Good

¹ O taste and see that the Lord is good;
happy are those
who take refuge in him.
² Happy are those
who keep his decrees,
who seek him with their whole heart.

³ For the law of the Lord is perfect,
reviving the soul;
the decrees of the Lord are sure,
making wise the simple.

⁴ The precepts of the Lord are right,
rejoicing the heart;
the commandment of the Lord is clear,
enlightening the eyes.

⁵ The fear of the Lord is pure,
enduring forever;
the ordinances of the Lord are true
and righteous altogether.

⁶ More to be desired are they than gold,
even much fine gold;
sweeter also than honey,
and the drippings of the honeycomb.

O Come, Let Us Worship and Bow Down

1 O come, let us worship
   and bow down,
   let us kneel before the Lord, our Maker!
2 For we are the people of his pasture,
   and the sheep of his hand.

3 Do not put your trust in princes,
   in mortals, in whom there is no help.
4 When their breath departs,
   they return to the earth;
   on that very day their plans perish.

5 Our help is in the name of the Lord,
   who made heaven and earth.
6 Great is our Lord,
   and abundant in power;
   his understanding is beyond measure.

7 His delight is not
   in the strength of the horse,
   nor his pleasure
   in the speed of the runner;
8 but the Lord takes pleasure
   in those who fear him,
   in those who hope in his steadfast love.

9 O come, let us worship
  and bow down,
  let us kneel before the Lord, our Maker!
10 For we are the people of his pasture,
  and the sheep of his hand.

Holy, Holy, Holy Is the Lord God of Hosts

1 O come and hear, all you who fear God;
   glorious is the Lord, and righteous.
2 The Lord is king,
   he is robed in majesty;
   the Lord is robed,
   he is girded with strength.

3 The heavens are telling the glory of God,
   and the firmament
   proclaims his handiwork.
4 Day to day pours forth speech,
   and night to night declares knowledge.

5 There is no speech, nor are there words;
   their voice is not heard.
6 Yet their voice goes out
   through all the earth,
   and their words to the end of the world.

7 More majestic than the waves of the sea,
   majestic on high is the Lord!
8 Holy, holy, holy is the Lord of hosts;
   the whole earth is full of his glory.

Be Glad in the Lord and Rejoice

1 Be glad in the Lord
and rejoice, O righteous,
and shout for joy,
all you upright in heart.
2 For the earth is the Lord's
and all that is in it,
the world, and those who live in it.
3 He spoke, and it came to be;
he commanded, and it stood firm.

4 O sing to the Lord,
sing praises to his name;
lift up a song,
be exultant before him.
5 If he tears down,
no one can rebuild;
if he shuts someone in,
no one can open up.
6 If he withholds the waters,
they dry up;
if he sends them out,
they overwhelm the land.

7 O sing to the Lord,
   bless his name;
   tell of his salvation
   from day to day.
8 Remember his wonderful works,
   his miracles,
   and the judgments he uttered.
9 Declare his glory
   among the nations,
   his marvelous works
   among all the peoples.

I Will Give Thanks to the Lord

1 I will give thanks to the Lord;
I will tell of all his wonderful deeds.
2 I will be glad and exult in him;
I will sing praises to his name.

3 How great are his signs;
how mighty his wonders!
His kingdom
is an everlasting kingdom,
his sovereignty
from generation to generation.

4 I will give thanks to the Lord;
I will tell of all his wonderful deeds.
5 I will be glad and exult in him;
I will sing praises to his name.

6 The Lord sits enthroned forever;
he has established
his throne for judgment.
7 He judges the world
with righteousness;
he judges the peoples with equity.

Sing Aloud to God Our Strength

1 O worship the Lord
   in holy splendor;
   tremble before him, all the earth.
2 Sing aloud to God our strength;
   raise a song,
   sound the tambourine.

3 O sing to the Lord a new song,
   for he has done marvelous things.
4 Long ago he laid
   the foundations of the earth,
   and the heavens
   are the work of his hands.

5 In his hand are
   the depths of the earth;
   the heights of the mountains
   are his also.
6 The sea is his, for he made it,
   and the land,
   which his hands have formed.

7 They will perish,
   but he endures.
   They will wear out like a garment.
8 But he is the same;
   his years have no end.

⁹ O worship the Lord
  in holy splendor;
  tremble before him, all the earth.
¹⁰ Sing aloud to God our strength,
  raise a song,
  sound the tambourine.

Sing to God, O Kingdoms of the Earth

1 Sing to God, O kingdoms of the earth;
   sing praises to the Lord.
2 Sing to the Lord a new song,
   his praise to the end of the earth.
3 For justice is the foundation
   of his throne,
   and steadfast love goes before him.

4 He shall judge between the nations,
   and shall arbitrate for many peoples;
   they shall beat their swords
   into plowshares,
   and their spears into pruning hooks;
   nation shall not lift up sword
   against nation,
   neither shall they learn war any more.

5 O praise the Lord, all you nations;
   extol him, all you peoples!
6 Great is his steadfast love toward us,
   and his faithfulness endures forever.

Bless Our God, O Peoples

1 Bless our God, O peoples,
  let the sound of his praise be heard.
2 Rejoice in the Lord, O you righteous,
  and give thanks to his holy name.

3 The Lord is the everlasting God,
  the Creator of the ends of the earth.
  He does not faint or grow weary;
  his understanding is unsearchable.
4 He gives power to the faint,
  and strengthens the powerless.

5 Even youths will faint and be weary,
  and the young will fall exhausted.
6 But those who wait for the Lord
  shall renew their strength,
  they shall mount up
  with wings like eagles,
  they shall run and not be weary,
  they shall walk and not faint.

Hear This, All You People

1 Hear this, all you people;
   give ear, all inhabitants of the world,
2 both low and high,
   rich and poor together.

3 In vain, you rise up early
   and go late to rest,
   eating the bread of anxious toil.
4 Unless the Lord builds the house,
   those who build it labor in vain.

5 O come and see what God has done;
   he is awesome
   in his deeds among mortals.
6 He heals the brokenhearted,
   and binds up their wounds.

7 Happy are those who fear the Lord,
   who greatly delight
   in his commandments.
8 They are not afraid of evil tidings;
   their hearts are firm,
   secure in the Lord.

⁹ They rise in darkness
   as a light to the upright;
   they are gracious, merciful,
   and righteous.
¹⁰ They have distributed freely;
   they have given to the poor.

IV
PSALMS OF PRAISE TO GOD

I Will Give Thanks to You, O Lord My God

1 I will give thanks to you,
   O Lord my God;
   I will glorify your name forever.
2 For your name, O God,
   like your praise,
   reaches to the ends of the earth.

3 I will sing of loyalty and justice;
   to you, O Lord, I will sing.
4 For you have been my help;
   in the shadow of your wings
   I sing for joy.

5 I will meditate on your precepts,
   and fix my eyes on your ways.
6 For all your commandments are right,
   and your decrees are very sure.

7 I will sing of your steadfast love,
  I will proclaim your faithfulness
  to all generations.
8 For you, O Lord,
  are good and forgiving,
  abounding in steadfast love
  to all who call on you.

9 I will tell of your name
  to my brothers and sisters;
  in the midst of the congregation
  I will praise you.
10 For you, O Lord, are the hope
  of the ends of the earth;
  with you is the fountain of life.

O Lord, You Are My Shepherd

1 O Lord, you are my shepherd;
   I shall not want.

2 You make me lie down
   in green pastures;
   you lead me beside still waters.

3 You restore my soul;
   you lead me in paths of righteousness
   for your name's sake.

4 Even though I walk
   through the darkest valley,
   I will fear no evil;
   for you are with me;
   your rod and your staff—
   they comfort me.

5 You prepare a table before me
   in the presence of my enemies;
   you anoint my head with oil;
   my cup overflows.

6 Surely, goodness and mercy
   shall follow me
   all the days of my life,
   and I shall dwell
   in your house, O Lord,
   my whole life long.

O Lord, How Manifold Are Your Works

1 O Lord, how manifold are your works!
  In wisdom you have made them all.
2 The heavens are yours,
  the earth also is yours;
  the world and all that is in it.

3 You stretch out the heavens;
  you set the earth on its foundation.
4 You make the gateways
  of the morning and the evening
  shout for joy.
5 You crown the year with your bounty;
  the pastures of the wilderness overflow.
6 The meadows clothe
  themselves with flocks;
  the valleys deck themselves with grain.

7 All your works
  shall give thanks to you, O Lord,
  and all your faithful shall bless you.
8 They shall speak
  of the glory of your kingdom,
  and tell of your power,
9 to make known to all people
  your mighty deeds,
  and the glorious splendor
  of your kingdom.

10 You, O Lord, have made me glad
   by your works;
   at the work of your hands
   I sing for joy.

How Precious, O God,
Is Your Steadfast Love

1 How precious, O God,
   is your steadfast love!
   All people may take refuge
   in the shadow of your wings.
2 They feast on the abundance
   of your house,
   and you give them drink
   from the river of your delights.

3 Happy are the people
   who know the festal shout,
   who walk in the light
   of your countenance;
4 they exult in your name,
   and extol your righteousness.

5 You are the glory of their strength;
   by your favor their horn is exalted.
6 When deeds of iniquity
   overwhelm them,
   you forgive their transgressions.

7 How precious, O God,
   is your steadfast love!
   All people may take refuge
   in the shadow of your wings.
8 O Lord my God,
   I will give thanks to you forever;
   I will exult and rejoice
   in your steadfast love.

I Love You, O Lord, My Strength

1 I love you, O Lord, my strength;
   you are my fortress and my deliverer;
   you are my God, my rock,
   in whom I take refuge;
   you are my shield,
   and the horn of my salvation.

2 The cords of death encompassed me;
   the torrents of perdition assailed me.
3 The cords of Sheol entangled me;
   the snares of death confronted me.

4 In my distress I called upon you;
   to you, my God, I cried for help.
   From your temple
   you heard my voice,
   and my cry to you reached your ears.

5 You reached down from on high;
   you drew me out of mighty waters.
6 When I was brought low,
   you saved me, O Lord;
   you delivered my soul from death.
7 You have turned my mourning
   to dancing, O Lord,
   and you have clothed me with joy.
8 For this, I will extol you,
   and sing praises to your name.

O Lord, My Soul Makes Its Boast in You

1 O Lord, my soul
    makes its boast in you,
      for you are a shield around me;
    you are my glory,
      and the one who lifts up my head.

2 Where can I go from your spirit?
    Or where can I flee
      from your presence?
3 If I take the wings of the morning
    and settle at the limits of the sea,
4 even there your hand shall lead me,
    and your right hand
      shall hold me fast.

5 O Lord, your steadfast love
    is better than life,
      therefore my lips will praise you.
6 I will bless you as long as I live;
    I will lift up my hands
      and call on your name.

7 My soul, O Lord,
    is satisfied as with a rich feast,
    and my mouth praises you
      with joyful lips.

O God, You Are My Refuge and Strength

1 O God, you are my refuge
    and strength,
    a very present help in trouble.
2 Therefore I will not fear,
    though the earth should change.

3 Though its waters roar and foam,
    I will not fear.
    Though the mountains tremble,
    I will not fear.

4 Though an army encamp against me,
    my heart shall not fear.
    Though wars rise up against me,
    yet I will be confident.

5 O Lord, you are my light
    and my salvation;
    whom shall I fear?
    You are the stronghold of my life;
    of whom shall I be afraid?

6 My heart is steadfast, O God,
    my heart is steadfast.
7 O my strength,
    I will sing praises to you,
    for you, O God, are my fortress.

How Majestic Is Your Name
in All the Earth

1 O Lord, my Sovereign,
   how majestic is your name
   in all the earth!

2 When I look at your heavens,
   the work of your fingers,
   the moon and stars
   that you have established—
3 what are human beings
   that you are mindful of us;
   what are mortals
   that you care for us?

4 You have made us
   a little lower than angels,
   and crowned us
   with glory and honor.
5 You have given us dominion
   over the works of your hands;
   you have put all things
   under our feet,
6 all sheep and oxen,
   and also the beasts of the field,
7 the birds of the air,
   and the fish of the sea,
   whatever passes along
   the paths of the seas.

⁸ O Lord, my Sovereign,
   how majestic is your name
   in all the earth!

Oh, How I Love Your Law, O Lord

1 Oh, how I love your law, O Lord!
  It is my meditation all day long.

2 How sweet are your words to my taste,
  sweeter than honey to my mouth.

3 The law of your mouth is better to me
  than thousands of gold and silver pieces.

4 Your word is a lamp to my feet
  and a light to my path.

5 Your decrees are my heritage forever;
  they are the joy of my heart.

6 Your statutes have been my song
  wherever I make my home.

7 My lips will pour forth praise,
  because you teach me your statutes.

8 My tongue will sing of your promise,
  for all your commandments are right.

O Lord, You Are My Chosen Portion

1 O Lord, you are my chosen portion;
  you are my strength and my might.
2 I will bless you at all times;
  your praise shall be in my mouth.

3 Though the fig tree does not blossom,
  and no fruit is on the vines,
  yet I will give thanks to you;
  I will sing praises to you.

4 Though the produce of the olive fails,
  and the fields yield no food,
  yet I will praise your name, O God;
  I will magnify you with thanksgiving.

5 Though the flock is cut off from the fold,
  and there is no herd in the stalls,
  yet I will rejoice in you, O Lord;
  I will exult in you, O God of my salvation.

I Will Extol You, My God and My King

¹ I will extol you, my God and my King,
  and bless your name forever and ever.
² On the splendor of your majesty
  and on your wondrous works,
  I will meditate, O God.
³ Every day I will bless you,
  and praise your name forever and ever.

⁴ You, O God, are most high
  over all the earth;
  you have set your glory
  above the heavens.
⁵ Your throne is established from of old;
  you are from everlasting.
⁶ You are clothed with honor and majesty,
  wrapped in light as with a garment.

⁷ Righteousness is the foundation
  of your throne,
  and steadfast love goes before you.
⁸ Your kingdom is an everlasting kingdom;
  your dominion endures
  through all generations.
⁹ I will extol you, my God and my King,
  and bless your name forever and ever.

You, O Lord, Are Enthroned Forever

1 O Lord, it is good to give thanks,
  to sing praises to your name,
  to declare your steadfast love
  and your faithfulness, O Most High.

2 Long ago you laid
  the foundation of the earth,
  and the heavens
  are the work of your hands.
3 They will perish, but you endure;
  they will all wear out like a garment.
  You change them like clothing,
  and they pass away.

4 But you are the same, O Most High,
  and your years have no end.
5 You, O Lord, are enthroned forever;
  your name endures to all generations.

READING THE PSALMS

The Book of Psalms contains two dominant types of poetry—the psalm of sorrow and the psalm of praise.

When life was affirmed or threatened by some significant event in ancient Israel, the community responded with appropriate forms of worship that gave rise to the psalm of sorrow or the psalm of praise.

When events such as drought or defeat in battle threatened the community, the Israelites would hold special fasts. During these solemn occasions, sacrifices were offered to God, and the people, dressed in sackcloth and ashes, would dramatize their plight through oral lamentation. The psalms of sorrow were born out of this oral dramatization of human lament.

The ingathering of crops and victory in battle were celebrated by special feasts that sanctified God's gifts of life and prosperity. During these joyous celebrations, small portions of the sacrificial animal were offered up by fire to God and the rest were consumed. Such feasts were the life-settings for what became the psalms of praise.

In light of the oral origins of the psalms, my objective in selecting, arranging, and editing the psalms in this book has been to create a collection that is appropriate for oral interpretation today.

The psalms are organized according to their literary form. Part one consists of psalms of sorrow. Part two contains psalms of praise. Both parts are divided into two sections. The first section of each part contains psalms addressed to humankind. The second consists of psalms addressed to God.

Reading the Psalms of Sorrow

The basic assumption underlying the psalm of sorrow is that suffering should be a shared experience. Rather than hiding their suffering, the psalm writers exposed their anguish both to God and to humankind in the most graphic language they could command.

In laments addressed to humankind, the objective of the psalmists is to call attention to their sorrow in such a way that those about them will respond empathetically to their plight. As poets, the psalmists crafted their sorrow into literary compositions that transcended their own suffering by grounding it in two fundamental notions: 1) there is indeed a tragic dimension to life and 2) no one should stand aloof from it.

By dramatizing their sorrow as an authentic human experience that deserves to be acknowledged, the psalmists elevated their laments to a redemptive level.

In psalms of sorrow addressed to God, the psalmists expected that the oral expression of their sorrow would draw God into their suffering in a redemptive way. In most but not all cases, they hoped for a reversal of their plight and so petitioned God for help. But regardless of the outcome, they did not turn their back on God, the ultimate source of their being. Through the boldness of their lament, the psalmists made God a participant in their suffering, and thereby they received the intrinsic catharsis that comes from sharing one's sorrow with God.

If we are truly sensitive to the plight of the psalmists, we will stand in their presence while they dramatize their sorrow. Then we will sit in the dust with them for a moment, acknowledging that suffering is not proportioned equally in this world. In the silence that follows, we will prepare ourselves to feel the sorrows of our own day and respond empathetically to those who suffer among us.

An empathetic response includes a genuine acknowledgment of the suffering, whether it is physical or mental or both. This authenticates the sorrow as an appropriate response to suffering. Platitudes are as worthless to those who suffer as no response at all.

These laments give us the poetic language to communicate our own sorrows in a dramatic way. Current conventions do not encourage us to express our sorrows to family or friends with intense feelings. Even in our prayers to God, we are taught to tiptoe around the anguish of our suffering. The only part of the lament that we have kept in our prayers is the petition for God's help. I am suggesting, however, that we can appropriate the intrinsic benefits of the psalms of sorrow for our own sufferings through dramatic, oral readings.

The rhetoric of suffering in some psalms of lament may be problematic for contemporary readers who make a distinction between what modern theologians call the intentional will of God (what God wants to happen) and the permissive will of God (what God permits to happen). The psalms of sorrow do not make such distinctions in their descriptions of suffering. Whatever happens is ultimately from the hand of God, regardless of what intermediate agents are involved.

Although I personally make a distinction between the intentional and permissive will of God, I appreciate and respect the perspective of Biblical poets who do not. In an inclusive and metaphorical sense, if something happens, it is ultimately from the hand of God whether he wanted it to happen or only allowed it to happen. This is how I read these texts.

In other laments, the psalmists realize that they may be facing death, which is described as going down to Sheol, the realm of the dead. Typically, the psalmists in this situation petition God to heal them and extend their life in the realm of the living. Atypically, the poet may express a loss of hope for life among the living (Job 7:6) but never a loss of belief in God.

Occasionally, the poet may express a readiness for death or even a longing for death as in Job 6:8-10:

O that I might have my request,
and that God would grant my desire;
That it would please God to crush me,
that he would let loose his hand and cut
me off!

I would even exult in unrelenting pain;
for I have not denied the words of the
Holy One.

The poet's longing for death in this passage may be too radical for some readers to appreciate. Others may find themselves in a position that enables them to identify fully with the sentiment. In any case, I believe that most readers can strengthen their own spirituality as they empathize with someone who realizes that death is approaching and it is time to die.

I have tried to create laments that express the widest range of sorrows and also the varied responses to them. Wherever possible, I have used texts with figurative language that has the greatest resonance for contemporary readers to express their own sorrow.

Reading the Psalms of Praise

The underlying assumption of the psalms of praise is that humans owe their existence to God, the one eternal source of all things. It is self-evident to the psalmists that we are neither eternal nor self-created. We thus owe our existence to something outside ourselves.

The psalmists extol the wonders of God both directly and indirectly as they direct their thoughts to God and to humankind. Although both forms of address occur frequently in the same psalm, they have different functions. I have thus selected, arranged, and edited the psalms in this volume with a single audience in mind. Each psalm is addressed either to humankind or to God but not both. Hopefully, this consistency will help contemporary readers better understand and appropriate the function of each form of address.

In the psalms addressed to humankind, the psalmists praise God indirectly by declaring his glory and majesty to other human beings. As such they function as a witness to the psalmists' faith in God. In addition to serving as witnesses to the psalmists' faith, the psalms also function as calls to worship.

Like the psalms of sorrow, psalms of praise addressed to humankind can be read in two ways—as the psalmists' witness to the reader and as the reader's own witness. In the former mode of reading, the psalmists confront us with their faith and in some cases call us to specific responses. Such readings can be especially helpful to us during our dark days of personal anguish. In our own existential loneliness, we often need to be reminded that it is both proper and beneficial for us to engage in worshipful praise to our creator. For we always transcend ourselves whenever we are able to praise our creator with true gratitude for our very existence, painful though it may be.

In psalms of praise that address God directly, the psalmists are actually engaged in worshipful praise and adoration of God. As in prayer, the psalmists are in direct communion with God.

These psalms can also be read in two ways. We can read them as examples of how the psalmists worshipped God. And we can appropriate them for our own worship of God. When we read them in the latter mode, we become the psalmists communing directly with God—the very ground of our being.

NOTES

I
PSALMS OF SORROW TO HUMANKIND

Is It Nothing to You, All You Who Pass By

  1 Lamentations 1:12
     Job 21:5
  2 Psalm 109:23
  3 Psalm 38:3
  4 Psalm 38:6
  5 Job 16:15
  6 Lamentations 1:12
     Job 21:5

My Heart Is Like Wine That Has No Vent

   1 Job 32:19
   2 Job 32:20
     Psalm 31:12
   3 Psalm 119:19
     Psalm 142:4
   4 Job 19:17
     Job 19:14
   5 Job 19:19
   6 Job 19:13
     Job 19:15
   7 Job 6:15
   8 Job 6:17
   9 Psalm 69:20
 10 Job 30:31

When I Waited for Light, Darkness Came

Truly the Thing I Fear Comes upon Me

O That My Vexation Were Weighed

1 Job 6:2
2 Job 6:3
    Job 7:11
3 Psalm 88:15
4 Psalm 32:4
5 Psalm 40:12
6 Job 16:6
7 Job 3:24
    Job 17:7
8 Psalm 4:6
    Psalm 39:13

My Days Are Past, My Plans Are Broken Off

1 Job 19:21
2 Job 6:4
3 Psalm 88:8
    Job 7:7
4 Job 19:21
5 Job 19:8
6 Job 9:25
7 Job 9:21
8 Job 19:9
9 Job 30:15
10 Job 19:21
11 Job 19:10
12 Jeremiah 8:18
    Job 17:11

My Eyes Are Weary from Looking Up

1 Job 34:2
2 Jeremiah 12:1
3 Psalm 10:3
    Psalm 17:10
4 Psalm 140:3
5 Psalm 55:15
    Psalm 36:2

How Lonely Sits the City

In the Noontide of My Days I Must Depart

The Grave Is Ready for Me

II
PSALMS OF SORROW TO GOD

How Long, O Lord? How Long?

Have Mercy upon Me, O God

7   Psalm 51:11
8   Psalm 51:16
9   Psalm 51:17
10 Psalm 51:2
11 Psalm 51:7

To You, O Lord, I Lift Up My Soul

1   Psalm 25:1
    Psalm 25:2
2   Psalm 130:1
    Psalm 123:1
3   Psalm 69:2
4   Psalm 119:143
    Psalm 119:28
5   Psalm 22:11
6   Psalm 144:7
7   Psalm 62:1
    Psalm 62:2
8   Psalm 130:6
9   Psalm 61:2
    Psalm 61:3
10 Psalm 61:4

My God, My God, Why Have You Forsaken Me

1   Psalm 22:1
2   Psalm 22:2
3   Psalm 116:3
4   Psalm 22:14
5   Psalm 22:15
6   Psalm 143:6
7   Psalm 22:9
8   Psalm 22:10
9   Psalm 27:9
10 Psalm 141:2
11 Psalm 22:19

Rise Up, O Lord

1 Psalm 9:19
  Psalm 17:6
2 Psalm 11:2
3 Psalm 7:14
4 Psalm 12:8
5 Psalm 10:7
6 Psalm 10:4
  Psalm 10:6
7 Psalm 10:2
  Psalm 10:8
8 Psalm 10:9
  Psalm 10:8
9 Psalm 10:1
10 Psalm 7:9
   Psalm 35:8
11 Psalm 10:12
   Psalm 10:15
12 Psalm 58:7

My Spirit Fails

1 Psalm 5:1
2 Psalm 28:2
  Psalm 6:4
3 Job 30:30
  Job 30:27
4 Psalm 88:3
5 Psalm 21:6
6 Psalm 16:16
7 Psalm 5:1
8 Psalm 143:7

In the Shadow of Your Wings

1 Psalm 31:1
  Psalm 38:21
2 Psalm 25:16

O Lord, How Long Shall the Wicked

I Would Not Live Forever

Teach Us to Number Our Days

1 Psalm 90:1
2 Psalm 90:2
3 Psalm 90:4
4 Psalm 90:10
5 Psalm 90:5
6 Psalm 90:6
7 Psalm 90:9
  Psalm 90:3
  Psalm 90:5
8 Psalm 90:12

O Prosper the Work of My Hands

1 Psalm 90:13
2 Psalm 90:7
3 Psalm 31:10
  Psalm 42:3
4 Psalm 90:9
5 Psalm 7:1
  Psalm 31:15
6 Psalm 90:14
7 Psalm 90:16
  Psalm 90:17

O Lord, All My Longing Is Known to You

1 Psalm 38:9
2 Psalm 25:4
  Psalm 119:176
3 Psalm 51:12
4 Psalm 43:3
5 Psalm 51:6
  Psalm 51:16
6 Psalm 51:10
7 Psalm 19:14
8 Psalm 38:15
9 Psalm 42:1

1 Psalm 139:1
2 Psalm 139:2
    Psalm 139:3
3 Job 31:21
    Job 31:16
4 Psalm 9:13
    Psalm 25:18
5 Job 31:19
6 Psalm 9:13
    Psalm 25:18
7 Job 31:29
8 Psalm 9:13
    Psalm 25:18
9 Job 31:5
10 Psalm 9:13
    Psalm 25:18
11 Job 31:7
12 Psalm 9:13
    Psalm 25:18
13 Psalm 4:1
14 Psalm 39:8
    Psalm 39:7

III
PSALMS OF PRAISE TO HUMANKIND

O Come, Let Us Sing to the Lord

1   Psalm 95:1
2   Psalm 95:2
3   Psalm 145:13
4   Psalm 145:18
5   Psalm 57:10
6   Psalm 65:3
7   Psalm 34:3
8   Psalm 89:52

The Lord Is My Shepherd

1   Psalm 23:1
2   Psalm 23:2
3   Psalm 23:3
4   Psalm 23:4
5   Psalm 23:5
6   Psalm 23:6

Make a Joyful Noise to the Lord

1   Psalm 100:1
   Psalm 100:2
2   Psalm 33:2
   Psalm 33:3
3   Psalm 100:3
4   Psalm 89:11
5   Psalm 100:4
6   Psalm 100:5

O Seek the Lord and His Strength

1   Psalm 105:4
2   Psalm 111:7
   Psalm 111:8

3 Psalm 119:130
4 Psalm 119:1
5 Psalm 1:1
6 Psalm 1:2
7 Psalm 105:4
8 Psalm 130:7
9 Psalm 145:8
Psalm 145:9
10 Psalm 106:3
11 Psalm 40:4
12 Psalm 1:2

The Lord Is My Chosen Portion

1 Psalm 16:5
Psalm 118:14
2 Psalm 34:1
3 Habakkuk 3:17
Psalm 57:9
4 Habakkuk 3:17
Psalm 69:30
5 Habakkuk 3:17
Habakkuk 3:18

Praise the Lord

1 Psalm 150:1
Psalm 150:2
2 Psalm 150:1
Psalm 150:2
3 Psalm 148:1
Psalm 148:7
4 Psalm 150:1
5 Psalm 148:2
6 Psalm 148:3
7 Psalm 148:11
Psalm 148:12

8   Psalm 148:11
    Psalm 148:12
9   Psalm 150:3
10 Psalm 150:4
11 Psalm 150:1
    Psalm 150:2
12 Psalm 150:1
    Psalm 150:2

God Is King of All the Earth

1   Psalm 47:1
2   Psalm 47:2
3   Psalm 95:4
4   Psalm 74:17
5   Psalm 74:16
6   Psalm 65:11
    Psalm 65:12
7   Psalm 65:13
8   Psalm 65:12
    Psalm 65:13
9   Psalm 47:1
10 Psalm 47:8
    Psalm 47:7

This Is the Day the Lord Has Made

1   Psalm 118:24
2   Psalm 118:4
3   Psalm 36:7
4   Psalm 36:8
5   Psalm 89:15
6   Psalm 89:16
7   Psalm 89:17
8   Psalm 65:3
9   Psalm 107:2
10 Psalm 106:1

O Taste and See That the Lord Is Good

1 Psalm 34:8
2 Psalm 119:2
3 Psalm 19:7
4 Psalm 19:8
5 Psalm 19:9
6 Psalm 19:10

O Come, Let Us Worship and Bow Down

1 Psalm 95:6
2 Psalm 95:7
3 Psalm 146:3
4 Psalm 146:4
5 Psalm 124:8
6 Psalm 147:5
7 Psalm 147:10
8 Psalm 147:11
9 Psalm 95:6
10 Psalm 95:7

Holy, Holy, Holy, Is the Lord God of Hosts

1 Psalm 66:16
  Psalm 116:5
2 Psalm 93:1
3 Psalm 19:1
4 Psalm 19:2
5 Psalm 19:3
6 Psalm 19:4
7 Psalm 93:4
8 Isaiah 6:3

Be Glad in the Lord and Rejoice

1 Psalm 32:11
2 Psalm 24:1
3 Psalm 33:9
4 Psalm 68:4

5 Job 12:14
6 Job 12:15
7 Psalm 96:2
8 Psalm 105:5
9 Psalm 96:3

I Will Give Thanks to the Lord

1 Psalm 9:1
2 Psalm 9:2
3 Daniel 4:3
4 Psalm 9:1
5 Psalm 9:2
6 Psalm 9:7
7 Psalm 9:8

Sing Aloud to God Our Strength

1 Psalm 96:9
2 Psalm 81:1
   Psalm 81:2
3 Psalm 98:1
4 Psalm 102:25
5 Psalm 95:4
6 Psalm 95:5
7 Psalm 102:26
8 Psalm 102:27
9 Psalm 96:9
10 Psalm 81:1
   Psalm 81:2

Sing to God, O Kingdoms of the Earth

1 Psalm 68:32
2 Isaiah 42:10
3 Psalm 89:14
4 Isaiah 2:4
5 Psalm 117:1
6 Psalm 117:2

Bless Our God, O Peoples

1 Psalm 66:8
2 Psalm 97:12
3 Isaiah 40:28
4 Isaiah 40:29
5 Isaiah 40:30
6 Isaiah 40:31

Hear This, All You People

1 Psalm 49:1
2 Psalm 49:2
3 Psalm 127:2
4 Psalm 127:1
5 Psalm 66:5
6 Psalm 147:3
7 Psalm 112:1
8 Psalm 112:7
9 Psalm 112:4
10 Psalm 112:9

IV
PSALMS OF PRAISE TO GOD

I Will Give Thanks to You, O Lord My God

1 Psalm 86:12
2 Psalm 48:10
3 Psalm 101:1
4 Psalm 63:7
5 Psalm 119:15
6 Psalm 119:172
   Psalm 93:5
7 Psalm 89:1
8 Psalm 86:5
9 Psalm 22:22
10 Psalm 65:5
   Psalm 36:9

O Lord, You Are My Shepherd

1 Psalm 23:1
2 Psalm 23:2
3 Psalm 23:3
4 Psalm 23:4
5 Psalm 23:5
6 Psalm 23:6

O Lord, How Manifold Are Your Works

1 Psalm 104:24
2 Psalm 89:11
3 Psalm 104:2
   Psalm 104:5
4 Psalm 65:8
5 Psalm 65:11
   Psalm 65:12
6 Psalm 65:13
7 Psalm 145:10
8 Psalm 145:11
9 Psalm 145:12
10 Psalm 92:4

How Precious, O God, Is Your Steadfast Love

1 Psalm 36:7
2 Psalm 36:8
3 Psalm 89:15
4 Psalm 89:16
5 Psalm 89:17
6 Psalm 65:3
7 Psalm 36:7
8 Psalm 30:12
   Psalm 31:7

I Love You, O Lord, My Strength

1 Psalm 18:1
  Psalm 18:2
2 Psalm 18:4
3 Psalm 18:5
4 Psalm 18:6
5 Psalm 18:16
6 Psalm 116:6
  Psalm 116:8
7 Psalm 30:11
8 Psalm 18:49

O Lord, My Soul Makes Its Boast in You

1 Psalm 34:2
  Psalm 3:3
2 Psalm 139:7
3 Psalm 139:9
4 Psalm 139:10
5 Psalm 63:3
6 Psalm 63:4
7 Psalm 63:5

O God, You Are My Refuge and Strength

1 Psalm 46:1
2 Psalm 46:2
3 Psalm 46:3
  Psalm 46:2
  Psalm 46:3
  Psalm 46:2
4 Psalm 27:3
5 Psalm 27:1
6 Psalm 57:7
7 Psalm 59:17

How Majestic Is Your Name in All the Earth

1 Psalm 8:1
2 Psalm 8:3
3 Psalm 8:4
4 Psalm 8:5
5 Psalm 8:6
6 Psalm 8:7
7 Psalm 8:8
8 Psalm 8:9

Oh, How I Love Your Law, O Lord

1 Psalm 119:97
2 Psalm 119:103
3 Psalm 119:72
4 Psalm 119:105
5 Psalm 119:111
6 Psalm 119:54
7 Psalm 119:171
8 Psalm 119:172

O Lord, You Are My Chosen Portion

1 Psalm 16:5
  Psalm 118:14
2 Psalm 34:1
3 Habakkuk 3:17
  Psalm 57:9
4 Habakkuk 3:17
  Psalm 69:30
5 Habakkuk 3:17
  Habakkuk 3:18

I Will Extol You, My God and My King

1 Psalm 145:1
2 Psalm 145:5
3 Psalm 145:2
4 Psalm 97:9
  Psalm 8:1

5 Psalm 93:2
6 Psalm 104:1
  Psalm 104:2
7 Psalm 89:14
8 Psalm 145:13
9 Psalm 145:1

You, O Lord, Are Enthroned Forever

1 Psalm 92:1
  Psalm 92:2
2 Psalm 102:25
3 Psalm 102:26
4 Psalm 102:27
5 Psalm 102:12